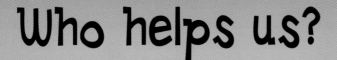

Who helps us?

In the street

Vic Parker

Little Nippers

www.heinemann.co.uk/library
Visit our website to find out more information about **Heinemann Library** books.

To order:
☎ Phone 44 (0) 1865 888066
🖹 Send a fax to 44 (0) 1865 314091
💻 Visit the Heinemann Bookshop at www.heinemann.co.uk/library to browse our catalogue and order online.

First published in Great Britain by Heinemann Library, Halley Court, Jordan Hill, Oxford OX2 8EJ, part of Harcourt Education.
Heinemann is a registered trademark of Harcourt Education Ltd.

Editorial: Jilly Attwood and Claire Throp
Design: Jo Hinton-Malivoire and bigtop, Bicester, UK
Models made by: Jo Brooker
Picture Research: Rosie Garai
Production: Séverine Ribierre

Originated by Dot Gradations
Printed and bound in China by South China Printing Company

ISBN 978 0 431 17322 1 (hardback)
08 07 06 05 04
10 9 8 7 6 5 4 3 2 1

ISBN 978 0 431 17327 6 (paperback)
08 07
10 9 8 7 6 5 4 3

British Library Cataloguing in Publication Data
Parker, Vic
In the street – (Who helps us?)
360
A full catalogue record for this book is available from the British Library.

Acknowledgements
The publishers would like to thank the following for permission to reproduce photographs:
David Hoffman p. **22–23**; Getty Images p. **9** (Michael Hart); Peter Evans Photography pp. **4**, **5**, **8**, **10**, **11**, **14**, **15**, **20**; Sally and Richard Greenhill p. **18**; Shout Pictures pp. **16**, **17**, **19**, **21**; Tudor Photography pp. **6–7**, **12**, **13**.

Cover photograph reproduced with permission of Photofusion

The publishers would like to thank Annie Davy for her assistance in the preparation of this book.

Every effort has been made to contact copyright holders of any material reproduced in this book. Any omissions will be rectified in subsequent printings if notice is given to the publishers.

Contents

Rise and shine!

It is early in the morning.

Most people are still asleep. Zzzzzzz!

Who brings letters to all the houses?

postal worker

Getting rid of rubbish

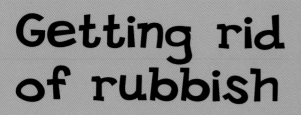

A big, noisy dustcart crawls along like a huge, **rumbling** monster.

The dustman throws rubbish inside it.

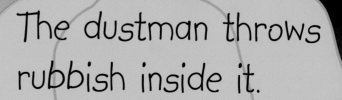

Taking a ride

This bus driver is helping lots of people get to school and work.

A taxi driver can take you wherever you want to go.

Taxi!

Busy traffic

A police officer helps the traffic flow.

A traffic warden keeps the street clear.

No parking here!

11

At work on the roads

Road workers fix problems down low ...

... and up high.

13

Keep moving!

Hello, new house!

removal man

Bye-bye, broken-down car!

car mechanic

15

To the rescue

Help! There has been an accident.

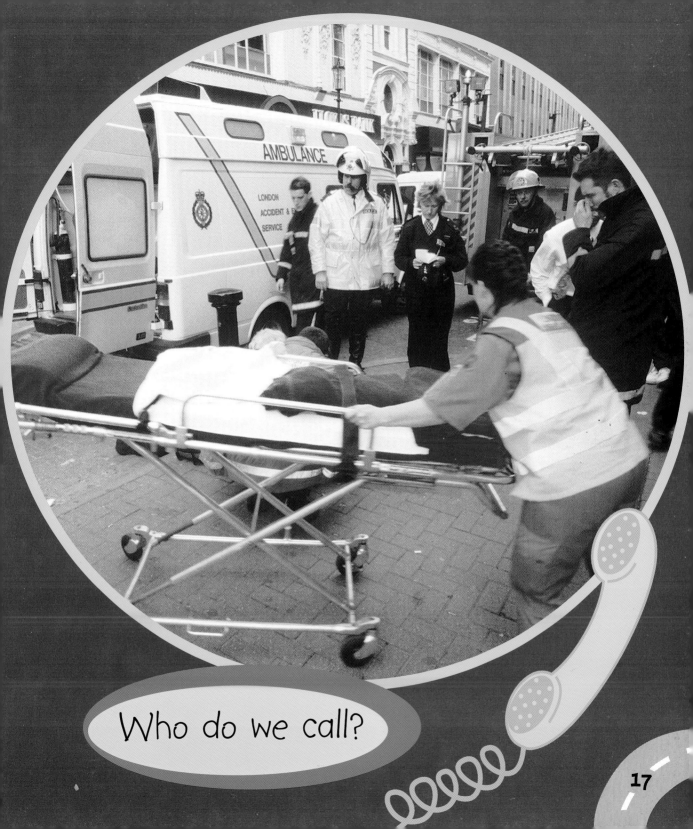

Who do we call?

Fire! Fire!

nee

nah

saxon

Speedy fire engine.

Brave firefighters.

Keeping the street clean

Is this driver's machine brushing away dirt?

Is this driver's machine clearing away snow?

Sleep tight!

Who looks after the street while you sleep?

Night-night!

Index

The end

Notes for adults

The *Who helps us . . .?* series looks at a variety of people that a young child may come across in different situations. The books explore who these people are, why we might interact with them, and how to communicate appropriately. Used together, the books will enable discussion about similarities and differences between environments and people, and encourage the growth of the child's sense of self. The following Early Learning Goals are relevant to this series:

Knowledge and understanding of the world
Early learning goals for a sense of place:
• show an interest in the world in which they live
• notice differences between features of the local environment
• observe, find out about and identify features in the place they live and the natural world
• find out about their environment, and talk about those features they like and dislike.

Personal, social and emotional development
Early learning goals for a sense of community:
• make connections between different parts of their life experience
• understand that people have different needs, views, cultures and beliefs, which need to be treated with respect.
Early learning goals for self-confidence and self-esteem:
• separate from main carer with support/confidence

• express needs and feelings in appropriate ways
• initiate interactions with other people
• have a sense of self as a member of different communities
• respond to significant experiences, showing a range of feelings when appropriate
• have a developing awareness of their own needs, views and feelings and be sensitive to the needs, views and feelings of others.

This book introduces the reader to a range of people they may come across when out and about. It will encourage young children to think about the jobs these people perform and how they help the community. **In the street** will help children extend their vocabulary, as they will hear new words such as *dustcart* and *traffic warden*. You may like to introduce and explain other new words yourself, such as *parking ticket* and *emergency services*.

Follow-up activities
• Make a model street with cardboard buildings, toy vehicles, and cut-out figures of the people who help us in this environment.
• Make some playing cards featuring people who help us in the street, such as firefighters, police officers, road workers, dustmen etc, for a game of 'Snap'.
• Take the children on a bus ride, playing 'I Spy' to spot any people who help us.